# TABLE OF CONTENTS

## ARE PREEMPTIVE ATTACKS MORALLY BANKRUPT?

> For centuries, international law recognized that nations need not suffer an attack before they can lawfully take action to defend themselves against forces that present an imminent danger of attack. Legal scholars and international jurists often conditioned the legitimacy of preemption on the existence of an imminent threat—most often a visible mobilization of armies, navies, and air forces preparing to attack. We must adapt the concept of imminent threat to the capabilities and objectives of today's adversaries.[1]

President George W. Bush, 43rd President of the United States of America, may have unintentionally established a new international standard for nation-states of the 21st century when he published *The National Security Strategy for the United States of America* in September 2002. Can "preemption" exist comfortably with "self-defense" when the topic is war? Can the concept of imminent threat, mentioned by President Bush, be adapted to allow a military response that until recently was solely considered prevention, rather than preemption? This paper will examine both the policy espoused in the National Security Strategy in general and the specific execution of that policy in Iraq in 2003. In particular, this paper will examine whether the policy and this specific execution are preemptive or preventive in nature, and whether they successfully pass the test of *Jus ad bellum* or "justice of war." The framework of this treatise will be straightforward. The first portion of the paper will provide definitions of critical terms, including current and historical international sources of important concepts related to the topic. The next section will examine the current administration's published documents and public policy statements from multiple sources that define United States preemptive policy in general and specifically preemptive actions in Iraq.

The remainder of the text will consider two major questions. First, is the US policy a preventive or preemptive policy? Second, is the policy ethically sound when examined using several criteria of the just war framework? To answer these questions, we will examine a number of reputable scholars' published views on these two questions. Finally, a conclusion based on the analysis in the body of the text will complete this paper.

### BACKGROUND

To effectively develop an evaluation of the United States security strategy of preemptive or preventive military action, it is first important to define a number of important terms and concepts. What truly makes this investigation so interesting is the lack of undisputed definitions for most of the critical ideas. In fact, the true issue, some would argue, lies in the definitions themselves. The key terms and concepts are: just-war moral/ethical framework, preemptive military action, preventive military action, right to self-defense, and imminent threat or danger.

JUST-WAR FRAMEWORK

A general ethical framework to evaluate national decisions about war is the "Jus ad bellum" (justice of war) criteria. Those just-war criteria are used to determine whether waging a war is justified, from a moral and ethical perspective. "The just-war tradition differs from pacifism in assuming that killing can sometimes be justified, e.g., in defense of the innocent. But just-war criteria also assume that war can be so destructive that the burden of moral proof is on those who would wage war. "[2] Just-war criteria rise from both religious and secular backgrounds. However both sources form a fairly consistent basis for just-war criteria. Depending on which authoritative source you choose to accept, the Jus ad bellum framework includes from four to seven criteria: just cause, legitimate authority, public declaration, right intention, proportionality, last resort, and reasonable hope of success. The most commonly accepted five do not include either public declaration or last resort as separate criteria. One can argue that these two criteria are sub-elements of other criteria – public declaration a subset of legitimate authority, and last resort a subset of proportionality. Right intention and reasonable hope of success, although important to the just-war framework, are not particularly relevant to this analysis of United States national policy. This paper will focus on only three criteria of the just-war framework: Legitimate Authority, Proportionality, and Just Cause. The greatest focus of international and national experts falls on Just Cause, because the definition of imminent threat plays so prominently in this specific criterion. The three criteria are defined below.

**Legitimate Authority**

Legitimate authority means that the decision to go to war was made by those authorized to do so, in accordance with national or international law. Proper authority typically resides in the sovereign power of the state and rests in specific people who can legally authorize the use of force. In some cases, this legal authority is blurred by internal differences. "In the American context, there is unresolved tension between the President as Commander in Chief and the authority of Congress to declare war."[3] In the United States, the authority to use force held by the President is different from the authority to declare war, held by Congress. This distinction can become a point of contention when considering just-war criteria. International treaties and customary law can also complicate the issue.

2

## Proportionality

Proportionality means that in weighing the value of the war, the probable positive outcome must be greater than the expected destruction that will be caused by the war. War must also be the last resort, after all other reasonable methods have failed.[4] It would be wrong for the objectives of war to exceed that which is necessary to restore the *status quo ante bellum* (that which existed prior to the war) unless the additional objectives are somehow tied to ensuring future problems are thus controlled. For example, was the carving and distribution of German land to Poland, France, and others at the end of World War I in agreement with the proportionality criteria? Probably not, although the allies argued that this action would ensure that Germany would not be a threat in the future, and disputed the idea that it was done to punish Germany and her people.

## Just Cause

"Possessing just cause is the first and arguably the most important condition of *jus ad bellum*."[5] This criterion is perhaps at the center of the definition quandary. It is on this definition, and the definitions of subordinate concepts that many just-war debates focus. "Just cause asks for a legitimate and morally weighty reason to go to war…the baseline standard in modern war thinking is *aggression*. States are justified in going to war to respond to aggression received. Classically, this means borders have been crossed in force."[6] Logically, the nation-state on the receiving end of aggression, which responds to an attack, is acting in self-defense. The great majority of just-war scholars recognize that self-defense is just cause. However, it is at this point that definitions begin to diverge and consensus breaks down.

In the framework of a preemptive war, instead of drawing on other generally recognized legitimate causes for armed intervention, such as humanitarian crises, this specific concept leads us to examine several words – aggression, self-defense, imminent, preemption, and prevention. What constitutes aggression that is adequate for a just cause military response? Broadly defined, aggression can encompass all the elements of national power - diplomatic, informational, military, or economic. Thus, self-defense could similarly be broad enough to include responses to a threatening use of national power. In 1941, for example, Japan's economic interests were threatened by the United States and Britain, as both countries cut off supplies of critical resources in response to Japan's military aggression in China. Japan chose to attack both the United States and Britain in early December 1941 because of our use of the economic element of national power. Few just-war theorists would conclude that Japan's actions met just cause. In fact, there are no historical examples of just cause responses to any other element of national power than military.  Although perhaps in the near future, that may no longer be the case.  So, selecting the appropriate bounds of aggression and self-defense, while clearly defining when danger is imminent is where the arguments begin.  Modern just-war theorists draw much of their arguments from historical precedent and customary law.  Let us examine some of these historical precedents to better define the bounds of the elements that combine to form the legitimate authority, proportionality, and just cause elements of the just-war criteria.

HISTORICAL PRECEDENTS

Although there are many historical precedents available that have helped to develop just-war theory over the centuries, we will examine three of the most notable: the work of Hugo Grotius, Daniel Webster's writing on the Caroline Incident between the United States and Britain in 1837, and the United Nations Charter, authored in 1945.

## Hugo Grotius

Hugo Grotius, who provided a secular view of just-war in the seventeenth century, is considered to be one of the originators of modern just-war theory.  His views on the just cause element of the just-war framework are included in great detail in his work, "On the Law of War and Peace."  Grotius asserts that

> the justifiable causes generally assigned for war are three, defence, indemnity, and punishment, all which are comprised in the declaration of Camillus against the Gauls, enumerating all things, which it is right to defend, to recover, and the encroachment on which it is right to punish.  There is an omission in this enumeration, unless the word recover be taken in its most extensive sense.  For recovering by war what we have lost, includes indemnity for the past, as well as the prosecution of our claim to a debt.[7]

Grotius' use of the word "defence" is vague, in that there are no bounds identified.  What criteria constitute defense is not clearly identified at this point in his book.  However, Grotius later states in three different locations of his work some clarifying thoughts.  "A just cause then of war is an injury, which though not actually committed, threatens our persons or property with danger."[8]  And then he states, "It has already been proved that when our lives are threatened with immediate danger, it is lawful to kill the aggressor, if the danger cannot otherwise be avoided."[9]  Finally, he states, "Among the causes assigned to justify war, we may reckon the commission of injury, particularly such as affects any thing which belongs to us."[10]  Grotius touches on several important aspects of just cause in these passages.  His first passage is consistent with the most basic understanding of just cause, and in agreement with the wording of the UN Charter, that defense, presumably against armed aggression, is an acceptable just cause. Additionally, Grotius addresses proportionality when he uses the phrase, "if the danger cannot otherwise be avoided." He is specifically addressing last resort as a component of proportionality. His argument contends that war can be justified when threatened with immediate danger, but that all other reasonable means must be exhausted first.

Grotius also expands his definition of just cause in these additional passages. First, he expands the definition to include action against an aggressor who threatens danger to either person or property prior to its occurrence. Then, he defines the right to kill the aggressor a bit more clearly by using the word "immediate" to describe danger that cannot be avoided in some other manner. Finally, he reaffirms that just war includes not only the commission of injury to a people, but to anything that belongs to that people. So, according to Grotius, just war includes preemptive actions against an aggressor who commits or in some way threatens to commit, not only physical injury to the people of the state, but also against the property or, by extension, the interests of that state.

## The Caroline Incident, 1837

A key concept raised by Grotius in his discourse is the idea of "immediate" danger. What does that really mean? Since Grotius's work, the more commonly used word has been "imminent" rather than "immediate." In its' simplest definition, imminent means, "about to occur; impending."[11] Additional definitions include "threatening to occur immediately; full of danger; threatening; menacing; perilous."[12] Finally, a usage definition comparing imminent, impending, and threatening identifies imminent as the strongest of the three and that "it denotes that something is ready to fall or happen on the instant. Impending denotes that something hangs suspended over us, and may so remain indefinitely; as, the impending evils of war. Threatening supposes some danger in prospect, but more remote; as, threatening indications for the future."[13] With this definition in mind, how did the Caroline Incident influence the thought of just-war theorists?

From a customary international law perspective, the most recognized source for the discussion of a first-strike armed attack comes from Daniel Webster, who was appointed as the United States Secretary of State in 1840. In response to a British attack on a US vessel, the Caroline, that was supplying munitions to insurgent Canadians in their struggle with the British Crown, Webster argued that the British attack was wrong. During his discourse, however, he laid out the criteria for armed first-strike attack. He stated, "It will be for that government to show a necessity of self-defense, instant, overwhelming, leaving no choice of means, no moment for deliberation."[14] This definition of preemptive attack clearly uses the important definition of imminent, specifically in his choice of words – "instant" and "no moment for deliberation." He argues effectively that pre-emptive self-defense is allowed in certain circumstances, just as Grotius does. Although he does not use the word "imminent" in his correspondence, he uses precisely the same word – instant – that matches our definition for imminent. Webster's definition of legal self-defense is tied very clearly to an imminent threat.

**United Nations Charter**

Within the legal arena, the most prominent example of an international standard for war is the United Nations Charter. The Charter defines what states can do, and what the collective United Nations can do with respect to armed conflict. Chapter VII of the United Nations Charter is entitled "Action With Respect to Threats to the Peace, Breaches of the Peace, and Acts of Aggression." This chapter contains articles 39 through 51. Article 51 of the United Nations Charter states, "Nothing in the present Charter shall impair the inherent right of individual or collective self-defence if an armed attack occurs against a Member of the United Nations, until the Security Council has taken measures necessary to maintain international peace and security."[15] This UN Charter article seems to address only a specific type of self-defense – self-defense against an armed attack. Examined by itself, it apparently does not address self-defense in any other situation.

However, Article 39 states, "The Security Council shall determine the existence of any threat to the peace, breach of the peace, or act of aggression and shall make recommendations, or decide what measure shall be taken in accordance with Articles 41 and 42, to maintain or restore international peace and security."[16] Article 42 states, "Should the Security Council consider that measures provided for in Article 41 [i.e., measures not involving the use of armed force] would be inadequate or have proved to be inadequate, it may take such action by air, sea, or land forces as may be necessary to maintain or restore international peace and security."[17] These two articles address collective defense against acts of aggression, **and** both threats to the peace and breaches of the peace. This is evidence that the United Nations does recognize that offensive military actions may be legitimate prior to an actual act of armed aggression - the right of multilateral self-defense must include threats to the peace, or something that is short of armed aggression.

There have been many examples of the United Nations authorizing action to maintain or restore international peace and security. In this context, examples of just cause could include "defense against an unjust invader, or humanitarian intervention to stop grave abuses of human rights by a tyrannical regime."[18]  Following that path, Article 51, which addresses the actions of individual states when faced with aggression, may not unequivocally restrict those same multilateral actions discussed in Article 39 – actions, military or not, to counter the existence of any **threat** to the peace.  There is at least an opening for that possible interpretation of the UN Charter.

Before considering these three sources, let us address one last set of definitions: preemptive and preventive.

### Preemptive And Preventive

Preemptive is defined as "a. relating to or constituting a military strike made so as to gain the advantage when an enemy strike is believed to be imminent; b. Undertaken or initiated to deter or prevent an anticipated, usually unpleasant situation or occurrence."[19]  Note that this definition links preemptive action with the critical word "imminent."  Preventive, on the other hand, is defined as, "Carried out to deter expected aggression by hostile forces."[20]  This definition is very similar to preemption, but lacks a key element – a link to time.  The definition has no element of time, and particularly, no use of the word "imminent" or, for that matter, impending or threatening.  There does not exist, in any source of either actual or customary law, any additional definition of these two words.  So, these dictionary definitions will suffice.  Preemption is a type of action that is tied to imminent self-defense.  It has an historical customary international law precedent.  Preventive military actions do not currently have any legal precedents to fall back on for justification.

### Analysis Of The Source Documents

Although there are numerous similarities between these documents, there are critical differences as well.  When considering causes for just war, Grotius lists several justifications for war, including, most importantly for this discussion, immediate danger.  We see that Daniel Webster gives additional detail to the definition of immediate, including "instant" and "no moment for deliberation."  Current scholars use the term "imminent" to fit these definitions, from which we derive the phrase "imminent threat."  According to both Grotius and Webster, an imminent threat may be just cause for preemptive war.  For many years, this was the acknowledged standard.  However, the United Nations Charter does not explicitly say that an individual state has the right to preemptive self-defense.  In fact, the only unilateral self-defense specifically mentioned in the Charter is self-defense against an armed attack.  The Charter allows more freedom for a collective response that could include threats to the peace, clearly leaving the option for a preemptive military action available.  In addition, there is a dichotomy between traditional views of imminent, which produce the aforementioned definition of preemptive war, and a potentially broader definition of imminent threat that could lead to preventive war.

This discrepancy between the historical just-war criteria, the existing international law, and the US desire to adapt the definition to include what many believe is preventive war is the focus of much debate and at the heart of this paper's concern. The United States Government NSS indicates that the definition of imminent needs to be adapted to fit the current threat environment.

An area of relative agreement between these documents is that of last resort as a part of proportionality. Grotius indicates that preemptive war against an imminent threat can be justified if all other reasonable attempts have failed. Webster also supports that idea when he uses the phrase "leaving no choice of means." Preemptive attack is justified in some cases, but you must have no other reasonable alternatives to that action. Finally, the United Nations Charter, which allows for the possibility of collective preemptive military action, focuses on the Security Council's determination of whether non-military actions have succeeded or will succeed, if tried. The UN Charter agrees with the Grotius and Webster on this subject – make certain that there are no other means to address the issue before resorting to armed military action.

Finally, Webster addresses legitimate authority when he mentions it will be "for that government to show" that preemptive attacks were justified, implying that the legitimate government, which has executed some military action, has already approved that action. The UN Charter, by its very nature as an international treaty, signed and ratified by legitimate governments, presumes that any action that is or is not taken in accordance with its stated Articles, is executed by a legitimate authority. Actions taken by an entity that was not the legitimate authority of a nation-state would not be bound to those rules, and discussion would be moot.

A final thought to consider in the just-war framework is the inter-relation between individual criteria. One example is the relationship between just cause and legitimate authority. If country X took a preemptive action against country Y, feeling that a threat was imminent, on the surface you could argue that just cause is met. However, if country X were a member of the United Nations, some would argue that any preemptive action, without approval of the Security Council, violates the UN Charter. If you support that argument, then the just cause action taken by country X violates the legitimate authority criterion because country X has broken an international treaty.

Now that we have reviewed the historical basis for just-war theory with respect to just cause, let us examine how the administration presents that argument through written and spoken policy.

## UNITED STATES GOVERNMENT POLICY ON PREEMPTION

On June 1, 2002, President George W. Bush provided the graduation speech for the newly commissioned officers of the United States Military Academy at West Point, New York. In this speech, President Bush first publicly discussed a United States military strategy of preemptive strikes against enemies of the United States. He begins his entry into this new policy by addressing the emergent threat of terrorism, specifically the events of September 11, 2001. The President stated, "In defending the peace, we face a threat with no precedent. The attacks of September the 11<sup>th</sup> required a few hundred thousand dollars in the hands of a few dozen evil and deluded men."[21] President Bush then addresses national military strategies this nation has used for many decades, and why these military strategies are not sufficient for today. He explained,

> For much of the last century, America's defense relied on the Cold War doctrines of deterrence and containment. In some cases, these strategies still apply. But new threats also require new thinking. Deterrence -- the promise of massive retaliation against nations -- means nothing against shadowy terrorist networks with no nation or citizens to defend. Containment is not possible when unbalanced dictators with weapons of mass destruction can deliver those weapons on missiles or secretly provide them to terrorist allies.[22]

President Bush then alludes to the idea of preemptive, or perhaps preventive military actions. He stated, "We cannot defend America and our friends by hoping for the best. If we wait for threats to fully materialize, we will have waited too long."[23] In these few sentences, President Bush ushers in a completely new public strategy for the use of United States military force. He continues in that same speech by saying, "Yet the war on terror will not be won on the defensive. We must take the battle to the enemy, disrupt his plans, and confront the worst threats before they emerge. In the world we have entered, the only path to safety is the path of action."[24] To this point in the speech, President Bush has not yet used the key word, "preemptive." However, just a few moments later he states, "Our security will require transforming the military you will lead -- a military that must be ready to strike at a moment's notice in any dark corner of the world. And our security will require all Americans to be forward-looking and resolute, to be ready for ***preemptive*** [highlighted by author] action when necessary to defend our liberty and to defend our lives."[25]  In just a few short minutes, President Bush quickly laid out a new military and national strategy and provided a justification for the policy as well. His next step was to make this policy an official part of our National Security Strategy.

In September 2002, President Bush published *The National Security Strategy of the United States of America*. In this document, President Bush addresses preemptive military action in the forward, using much the same rhetoric he used in the United States Military Academy graduation speech. He wrote, "And, as a matter of common sense and self-defense, America will act against such emerging threats before they are full formed."[26] His meaning is clear, although he does not use either preemptive or preventive. However, in section III of the document, *Strengthen Alliances to Defeat Global Terrorism and Work to Prevent Attacks Against Us and Our Friends*, President Bush wrote,

> We will disrupt and destroy terrorist organizations by: defending the United States, the American people, and our interests at home and abroad by identifying and destroying the threat before it reaches our borders. While the United States will constantly strive to enlist the support of the international community, we will not hesitate to act alone, if necessary, to exercise our right of self-defense by acting preemptively against such terrorists, to prevent then from doing harm against our people and our country.[27]

With this statement in the National Security Strategy, President Bush has changed the nature of how military forces may be used for the defense of the United States.

However, does the fact that the current administration used the word preemptive to describe these potential military actions make those actions preemptive? Cannot it be argued that these actions, as defined in the text of both the President's graduation speech at West Point and the National Security Strategy are not preemptive, but preventive? President Bush argues that we must change our concept of imminent threat based on the threats of today's world and, by altering that definition, which historically has been understood to support preemptive actions that are closely linked in time with immediate threat, actually allow preventive military actions as an additional element of national strategy. Never in the past have preventive military actions been justified using either legal or just-war criteria. Many nation-states have taken preventive military actions in the past, or at least defended an action in that manner, but without ever gaining the approval of the international community for the action.

By way of addressing the adaptation of imminent threat to the current environment, Deputy Secretary of Defense Paul Wolfowitz stated in a speech at the International Institute for Strategic Studies on December 2, 2002: "[T]he notion that we can wait to prepare assumes that we know when the threat is imminent. ... When were the attacks of September 11 imminent? Certainly they were imminent on September 10, although we didn't know it. ... Anyone who believes that we can wait until we have certain knowledge that attacks are imminent has failed to connect the dots that led to September 11."[28] This explanation is the key factor in the Bush administration's argument that imminent must be expanded, and preemptive become preventive when necessary. With that adaptation, preventive war could potentially satisfy just cause.

President Bush also addresses the second criteria - proportionality - in the just-war framework, (and in this case the last resort element). First, he indicates that containment and deterrence practices, which were effective during the cold war, are not effective against this new threat of terrorism. It appears that he is justifying armed military preventive action as a last resort before the future events actually play out. But later, he clarifies US intent by stating, "The United States will not use force in all cases to preempt emerging threats, nor should nations use preemption as a pretext for aggression."[29] President Bush has concluded that preemptive action may be required in some circumstances as a last resort, and that US policy will not be to act preemptively in every situation. His meaning is clear – the US will continue to adhere to the basic proportionality criteria espoused in just-war theory, so that any preemptive action will be a last resort response to an imminent threat.

So, in the context of this policy, where do the United States military actions against the regime of Saddam Hussein fall? Was that action preemptive or preventive? Was it a last resort? And was the action legal or ethical in the just-war framework? Let us now examine some substantial arguments presented by learned authors that evaluate the US policy and the intervention in Iraq specifically.

**EXPERT OPINIONS.**

The two elements of focus for this paper are an evaluation of whether the general US National Security Strategy and the specific action in Iraq are in agreement with particular criteria of the just-war framework. The criteria of Just Cause and Proportionality have applicability in both the conceptual side of the discussion, that of the policy itself, and the execution of the policy, the US military action in Iraq. The legitimate authority criteria, however, will often not have real meaning in the abstract of policy, for we assume that the legitimate authority *will* authorize use of force, when we are speaking about a group of potential events in the future. And, we assume that the legitimate authority of the state will not violate statutory or customary international law. However, for specific examples of that military force, legitimate authority is a valuable and necessary criterion to discuss. For this reason, we will examine just cause and proportionality with respect to the US policy and all three criteria with respect to the US action in Iraq. Below, we will consider some expert opinions on these various issues.

11

## LEGITIMATE AUTHORITY

We assume that legitimate authority will exist for an action when a policy is developed and articulated, such as the preemptive policy detailed in the National Security Strategy. However, legitimate authority must exist for each and every instance of that policy's execution. For the military intervention in Iraq, many were openly skeptical of President Bush's specified intent to take unilateral action against Iraq, without having Congressional approval of that action. Prior to any action by Congress, Joyce Appleby and Ellen Carol DuBois published an article entitled "War Issue Imperils Constitution," addressing the preemption policy using the legitimate authority criterion of the just-war framework. The authors state, "Article 1, Section 8 of the Constitution is explicit in giving Congress, not the president, the power to declare war. There's no ambiguity here concerning the original intent."[30] The authors logically identify that in an anticipated attack on Iraq, without Congressional declaration of war, the legitimate authority, by our own law, has failed to "legitimize" the war, and by extension, the preemptive attack. Later in the article the authors make the following claim: "The trauma of Sept. 11 attacks may have numbed the public to how unprecedented a preemptive attack from the United States would be. It would violate every principle this country has stood for."[31] A final slap at the NSS policy states their view quite clearly, "Failure to respect the Constitution by going to war on the president's say-so, without provocation, would rob American military action of all legitimacy."[32] The authors attempt to refute the preemptive policy on legitimate authority grounds, but that argument can only prevail if Congress fails to endorse the President's specific actions in time of conflict. In this case, Congress granted internal state legitimate authority by a vote of 77-23 authorizing war with Iraq in October 2002.

However, it is important to consider international and customary law as well. This point is extremely open to debate. Few would argue that Iraq heeded UN Security Council Resolution 1441. This resolution offered Iraq a final opportunity to comply with its disarmament obligations or it would face serious consequences.[33] From this perspective, it is possible to argue that the US led action in Iraq did have a degree of international legitimacy. Of course, others would argue that the US led effort did not have the *specific* approval of the UN Security Council, and so was not legitimate. From a just-war criterion of legitimate authority, the military intervention in Iraq was more likely valid than not.

## PROPORTIONALITY

The most important element of this criterion is the idea of last resort. War must be the last option after all other reasonable options have been exhausted. From a policy standpoint, a view

12

of last resort is important only from a stated intent perspective, since one can only determine if an action was a last resort after the fact, and even that can be problematic. So, from the policy perspective we have seen that the administration does promote preemptive war as a last resort and only in specific cases. The President does not argue that preemptive war is, nor should be, a common event that is authored by the United States or any other state. So, for the policy, we can say that the last resort criterion of the just-war framework is valid.

Next, we look to the actual intervention in Iraq. Was the military action a last resort? Could other avenues, not yet tried, have been used to solve the problem? Could other avenues that we were trying be continued with a hope of greater success? These are truly difficult questions. Those who argue that the war was not a last resort point to the potential to continue sanctions, to continue UN weapons inspections, and to continue pressing the Iraqi government for changes to how they responded to UN resolutions. Those who believe that the war was a last resort point to Iraq's violation of UN Resolution 1441 of 8 November 2002, which specified that this was, "a final opportunity to comply with its disarmament obligations."[34] Iraq failed to comply with this resolution, thereby using its last chance. Using that specific failure as the basis of the argument, the war against Iraq was a last resort, for Iraq failed to make good during its final opportunity. Additionally, others would argue that Iraq's repeated failure to respond to any of the sanctions, inspectors, and other behavior modifying activities showed that continued similar actions would have no noticeable effect. Thomas Nichols, in an article entitled, "Just War, Not Prevention," states, "In a repeating pattern, Iraq is served notice with resolutions, agrees to them, and then breaks them. The noncompliance with weapons inspections is just the most obvious example, but the point is that Saddam has now established, permanently and by his own doing, that he can never be trusted, and that no agreement with him now or in the future has any realistic hope of being observed."[35] The President and his administration have judged that Saddam's past behavior are indicative of his future behavior.

The real difficulty in this particular case is that we cannot know what Saddam would have done had we continued to execute the non-military actions against his regime. We can only guess, although based on his past actions mentioned earlier, it is easier to feel comfortable with a guess that he would never obey international obligations. For this instance, the President guessed that any additional activities would not have any effect, so war was the last resort. While you can argue either side of this, you cannot disprove that war was, in this case, a last resort.

JUST CAUSE

First, let us consider the just cause criterion with respect to US policy and the Iraq war. Anthony Arend relates in an article entitled, "International Law and the Preemptive Use of Military Force," that there are two clear groups of thought with regard to use of force, when considering the intent of the UN Charter.[36] He states, "On one hand, some commentators – 'restrictionists' we might call them – claim that the intent of Article 51 was explicitly to limit the use of force in self-defense to those circumstances in which an armed attack has actually occurred. ... 'Counterrestrictionists' would claim that the intent of the charter was not to restrict the preexisting customary right of anticipatory self-defense."[37] But based on the earlier discussion, it is clear that there are actually three groups of thought: those that do not recognize preemptive self-defense, those that recognize it in the traditional sense, and those that advocate an expanded view of preemptive self-defense, based on an expansion of the definition of imminent threat. Those in the first group agree fully with the UN Charter interpretation that no right to anticipatory self-defense exists. Representative of that group is Gu Guoliang, of the Chinese Academy of Social Sciences in Beijing.

In an article entitled "Redefine Cooperative Security, Not Preemption," Gu Guoliang states, "A national security strategy of preemption poses a serious challenge to the existing tenets of international law and to the framework of the UN."[38] Later, Guoliang states, "No country is entitled to deprive the UN of its right to judge whether or not a war is justified. The international community as a whole, therefore, cannot accept preemption as the national security strategy of one single nation. Otherwise, any single nation may become the judge and jury of international law."[39] Here is an example of where legitimate authority and just cause overlap. Guoliang may be arguing that the US violated legitimate authority because they had no UN Security Council approval for their action, or he may be arguing that no just cause exists because he does not agree with the President's interpretation of the UN Charter. For this discussion, we will interpret his argument to be against just cause, rather than legitimate authority. This group supports the existing international legal document, the UN Charter, in its strictest interpretation. From their position, the US policy of preemption is illegal, whether it is linked to the historical interpretation of preemption or not. In this group's opinion, the US policy fails just cause. As well, any action by the US that is based on this policy, such as our military action against Iraq, also fails just cause. Juan Alsace represents the views of the second group.

Alsace, in his article "In Search of Monsters to Destroy: American Empire in the New Millennium," addresses preemption in the context of American Imperialism. In doing so, he uses the just cause criterion of the just-war framework. Alsace notes that "preemption is not so

14

radical a concept; at heart it is simply self-defense."[40] Alsace's comments seem to support the preemptive policy as ethically correct. This opinion is in agreement with Grotius and Webster, but not necessarily the UN Charter. However, his next statement identifies his concern. "Controversy lies, however, in the robust version of self-defense espoused in the NSS. Therein preemption has moved from the classic, internationally recognized 'anticipatory self-defense' in the face of imminent danger to a flat assertion that the United States can even change regimes in order to obviate dangers not yet operational, as exemplified by the war against Iraq."[41] His argument is clearly against the policy, using the criterion of just cause, invoking the violation of "imminent threat" as the cornerstone of his argument. In Alsace's opinion, both the policy and the US intervention in Iraq fail the just cause criterion. Anthony Arend represents the third group.

In his article, "International Law and the Preemptive Use of Military Force," Arend presents a set of arguments that support both a preemptive and preventive interpretation of the United States NSS policy, and, by extension, just cause. Arend first argues that the United Nations Charter, the current international basis for analyzing military actions, is inadequate to address the international threats of today. He argues that the framework of the UN Charter does not address the two key elements that are the heart of the US NSS, Weapons of Mass Destruction and terrorism.[42] He asserts, "Neither WMD nor terrorist actors were envisioned in this framework."[43] He correctly points out that the US atomic weapons program was secret until the use of those weapons in August 1945. The UN Charter was developed during the spring of 1945, several months before our bombs were dropped on Hiroshima and Nagasaki. Arend notes, "as John Foster Dulles would later observe, the UN Charter was a 'pre-atomic' document."[44]

Arend continues with his discussion by pointing out the critical difference between conventional military threats and those of WMD and terrorism. Although conventional military actions provide warning of an imminent threat, based on troop movements, equipment preparation, and the like, these new threats are different.[45]

> It can be very difficult to determine whether a state possesses WMD, and by the time its use is imminent, it could be extremely difficult for a state to mount an effective defense. Similarly, terrorists use tactics that may make it all but impossible to detect an action until it is well underway or even finished. As a consequence, it could be argued that it would make more sense to target known WMD facilities or known terrorist camps or training areas long in advance of an imminent attack if the goal is to preserve the state's right to effective self-defense.[46]

15

Arend's argument, using the just war framework, is consistent with President Bush's contention in the NSS that the existing customary law definitions for military action in self-defense are insufficient to address today's problems. His argument is that both preemption and prevention can be consistent with just cause, when the definition is correctly expanded to recognize current threats. While this argument neatly sidesteps the existence of current international law by declaring it incomplete, it does follow a logical path to its conclusion. The argument does not, however, address customary law, such as presented by Grotius or Webster. The danger, of course, lies in the details of how a legitimate authority identifies when the new "rules" have been met.

The key difference between these three arguments is, not surprisingly, in the interpretation of self-defense and of imminent threat. Restrictionists claim that both the US policy and action in Iraq violate the United Nations Charter, Article 51, which does not recognize unilateral self-defense against anything but an armed act of aggression. While the UN Charter recognizes the option of a collective United Nations preemptive/preventive military action, unilateral actions are forbidden. The second group loudly protests the administration attempts to tie current US policy to historical precedents such as the Caroline incident in 1837, with Daniel Webster's ensuing discussion of legal preemption. They reject ties to Hugo Grotius, who also advocated preemptive attacks in certain time-sensitive situations. They believe that our policy and our action in Iraq violate the definition of imminent threat.

Those who support the US policy of preemption/prevention, including the current US administration, do not contest the existing international law or customary law. But, they contend rather vigorously that the existing framework cannot adequately address the threats of terrorism and WMD. They contend that when the UN Charter was developed, these problems did not exist. The point of this discourse is that President Bush's NSS policy, which calls for an adaptation of the concept of imminent threat, must occur if our nation is to continue to protect the security and freedom we so dearly hold.

So, which argument is compelling? From a just cause perspective, the policy may violate both international law and customary international law. Those who make these arguments are correct. However, to take this view is to ignore the one most important lesson of history – those who fight the last war, lose. President Bush and his administration have advocated through the NSS, a look to the present and to the future with regards to our national security needs. The President tossed the current framework aside, preserved the parts of it that are still viable, and created a new framework that gives us options to take action when it is needed to counter threats of this century. This path is dangerous, however, without international support. It is

16

imperative that the US continues to energetically work with our international brothers to slowly gain, if not approval, then at least acceptance, that preemptive and preventive military actions are sometimes necessary to ensure world stability. Very few laws, national or international are static. They change over time to recognize the reality of the times. President Bush's NSS policy and the US action in Iraq are correct, for now.

## CONCLUSION

After examining extensive arguments on all sides of the issue, and judging arguments on both sides of the just-war framework, I believe that the US policy and the US military intervention in Iraq are both correct. However, I believe that both of these actions violate customary international just-war theory, and may violate current statutory international law in the form of the UN Charter. Nevertheless, I am convinced that despite this violation, the policy and action are correct, for the existing framework of international law is not adequate to address the complexity of today's threat. It is time for both international law and just-war theory to advance and change, as they have over time to arrive at their current structure. The nature of our world has changed sufficiently that the old way of looking at things is no longer adequate. It is necessary to change our way of thinking as well.

WORD COUNT= 7441

# ENDNOTES

[1] George W. Bush, *The National Security Strategy of the United States of America* (Washington, D.C.: The White House, September 2002), 15.

[2] David L. Perry, "Just War Criteria and the War in Iraq"; 25 March 2003, 1.

[3] Martin L. Cook, "Ethical Issues in War: An Overview", in *U.S. Army War College Guide to Strategy*, ed. Joseph R. Cerami and James F. Holcomb, Jr. (Carlisle Barracks: U.S. Army War College, Strategic Studies Institute, 2001), 25.

[4] Ibid., 26.

[5] Alex Moseley, "Just War Theory", The Internet Encyclopedia of Philosophy, 2001; available from <http://www.utm.edu/research/iep/j/justwar.htm>; Internet; accessed 7 February 2004.

[6] Cook, 24.

[7] Hugo Grotius, *On the Law of War and Peace*, trans. A.C. Campbell (n.p.: Batoche Books, 2001), Book II, Chapter I, Section II; available from <http://socserv.socsci.mcmaster.ca/econ/ugcm/3113/grotius/law2.pdf>; Internet; accessed 9 February 2004.

[8] Ibid.

[9] Ibid., Book II, Chapter I, Section III.

[10] Ibid., Book II, Chapter II, Section I.

[11] *The American Heritage Dictionary of the English Language*, 4th ed. (n.p.: Houghton Mifflin Company, 2000); available from <http://dictionary.reference.com/search?q=imminent>; Internet; accessed 14 February 2004.

[12] *Webster's Revised Unabridged Dictionary* (n.p.: MICRA, Inc., 1998); available from <http://dictionary.reference.com/search?q=imminent>; Internet; accessed 14 February 2004.

[13] Ibid.

[14] History News Network Staff, "Would Daniel Webster Approve of an Attack on Iraq?", 8 October 2002; available from <http://hnn.us/articles/1024.html>; Internet; accessed 14 February 2004.

[15] *Charter of the United Nations*, 26 June 1945; available from <http://www.un.org/aboutun/charter/chapter7.htm>; Internet; accessed 27 Jan 2004.

[16] Ibid.

[17] Ibid.

[18] Perry, 1.

[19] *The American Heritage Dictionary of the English Language*.

[20] Ibid.

[21] George W. Bush, "President Bush Delivers Graduation Speech at West Point," 1 June 2002; available from <http://www.whitehouse.gov/news/releases/2002/06/20020601-3.html>; Internet; accessed 8 September 2003.

[22] Ibid.

[23] Ibid.

[24] Ibid.

[25] Ibid.

[26] Bush, *The National Security Strategy of the United States of America*, Foreword.

[27] Ibid., 6.

[28] Paul Wolfowitz, speech, Arundel House, London, England, International Institute for Strategic Studies, 2 December 2002; available from <http://www.defenselink.mil/speeches/2002/s.20021202-depsecdef.html>; Internet; accessed 4 March 2004.

[29] Bush, *The National Security Strategy of the United States of America*, 15.

[30] Joyce Appleby and Ellen Carol DuBois, "War Issue Imperils the Constitution," *The Los Angeles Times*, 17 September 2002, p. 13.

[31] Ibid.

[32] Ibid.

[33] Department of State, "UN Security Council Resolution 1441: Security Council Tightens Iraqi Disarmament Regime", press release, 8 November 2002; available from <http://usinfo.state.gov/topical/pol/terror/02110803.htm>; Internet; accessed on 1 March 2004.

[34] Ibid.

[35] Thomas M. Nichols, "Just War, Not Prevention," *Ethics and International Affairs* 17, no. 1 (2003): 25.

[36] Anthony Clark Arend, "International Law and the Preemptive Use of Military Force," *The Washington Quarterly* 26 (Spring 2003): 92.

[37] Ibid.

[38] Gu Guoliang, "Redefine Cooperative Security, Not Preemption," *The Washington Quarterly* 26 (Spring 2003): 137.

[39] Ibid., 138.

[40] Juan A. Alsace, "In Search of Monsters to Destroy:  American Empire in the New Millennium," *Parameters* 33 (Autumn 2003): 123.

[41] Ibid.

[42] Arend, 97.

[43] Ibid.

[44] Ibid.

[45] Ibid., 98.

[46] Ibid.

# BIBLIOGRAPHY

Alsace, Juan A. "In Search of Monsters to Destroy: American Empire in the New Millennium." *Parameters* Volume 33 (Autumn 2003): 122-129.

*The American Heritage Dictionary of the English Language*, 4th ed. n.p.: Houghton Mifflin Company, 2000. Available from <http://dictionary.reference.com/search?q=imminent>. Internet. Accessed 14 February 2004.

Appleby, Joyce, and Ellen Carol DuBois. "War Issue Imperils the Constitution." *The Los Angeles Times*, 17 September 2002, p. 13.

Arend, Anthony Clark. "International Law and the Preemptive Use of Military Force." *The Washington Quarterly* 26 (Spring 2003): 92-98.

Bush, George W. *The National Security Strategy of the United States of America.* Washington, D.C.: The White House, September 2002.

_____. "President Bush Delivers Graduation Speech at West Point." 1 June 2002. Available from <http://www.whitehouse.gov/news/releases/2002/06/20020601-3.html>. Internet. Accessed 8 September 2003.

Byrd, Robert C. "The War Debate." *The Los Angeles Times*, 9 October 2002, p. 15.

*Charter of the* United *Nations*. 26 June 1945. Available from <http://www.un.org/aboutun/charter/chapter7.htm>. Internet. Accessed 27 Jan 2004.

The Constitution of the United States. Available from http://www.usconstitution.net/const.txt>. Internet. Accessed 8 September 2003.

Cook, Martin L. "Ethical Issues in War: An Overview." In *U.S. Army War College Guide to Strategy*, ed. Joseph R. Cerami and James F. Holcomb, Jr., 25. Carlisle Barracks: U.S. Army War College, Strategic Studies Institute, 2001.

_____. "Moral Foundations of Military Service." *Parameters*, Volume 30 (Spring 2000): 117-129.

Guoliang, Gu. "Redefine Cooperative Security, Not Preemption." *The Washington Quarterly* 26 (Spring 2003): 137-138.

Grotius, Hugo. *On the Law of War and Peace*. Translated by . A.C. Campbell. N.p.: Batoche Books, 2001. Available from <http://socserv.socsci.mcmaster.ca/econ/ugcm/3113/grotius/law2.pdf>. Internet. Accessed 9 February 2004.

Herson, Lawrence J.R. "The Politics of Ideas: The American Political Culture: Do's and Don'ts of Political Life." In *The Politics of Ideas: Political Theory and American Public Policy.* Homewood, IL: Dorsey Press, 1984.

History News Network Staff. "Would Daniel Webster Approve of an Attack on Iraq?" 8 October 2002. Available from <http://hnn.us/articles/1024.html>. Internet. Accessed 14 February 2004.

Moseley, Alex. "Just War Theory." In *The Internet Encyclopedia of Philosophy*, 2001. Available from <http://www.utm.edu/research/iep/j/justwar.htm>. Internet. Accessed 7 February 2004.

Nichols, Thomas M. "Just War, Not Prevention." *Ethics and International Affairs* 17, no. 1 (2003): 25.

Nuechterlein, Donald E. "Defining U.S. National Interests: An Analytical Framework." In *America Recommitted: United States National Interest in a Restructured World.* Lexington: University Press of Kentucky, 1991.

Perry, David L. "Just War Criteria and the War in Iraq." 25 March 2003.

_____. "Ethics and War in Comparative Religious Perspectives." March 2003.

Schmitt, Gary, and Tom Donnelly. "The Bush Doctrine." Memorandum for Opinion Leaders. 30 January 2002. Available from <http://www.newamericancentury.org/defense-20020130.htm>. Internet. Accessed 8 September 2003.

Thomas, Evan. "Robert Kennedy: His Life." *Newsweek*, 14 August 2000, 250-260.

U.S Department of State. "UN Security Council Resolution 1441: Security Council Tightens Iraqi Disarmament Regime." Press Release. 8 November 2002. Available from <http://usinfo.state.gov/topical/pol/terror/02110803.htm>. Internet. Accessed on 1 March 2004.

*Webster's Revised Unabridged Dictionary*. N.p.: MICRA, Inc., 1998. Available from <http://dictionary.reference.com/search?q=imminent>. Internet. Accessed 14 February 2004.

Wolfowitz, Paul. Speech. Arundel House, London, England, International Institute for Strategic Studies, 2 December 2002. Available from <http://www.defenselink.mil/speeches/2002/s.20021202-depsecdef.html>. Internet. Accessed 4 March 2004.